Love and the Eye

For Allan Aycock

Kore Press First Book Award winner | Claudia Rankine, judge

Love and the Eye

Laura Newbern

KORE PRESS | TUCSON | 2010

Kore Press, Inc.
Tucson, Arizona USA
www.korepress.org

Copyright © 2010 Kore Press

Library of Congress cataloging-in-publication data:

   Newbern, Laura, 1964-
    Love and the eye / Laura Newbern.
      p. cm.
      Poems.
      ISBN 978-1-888553-34-5 (alk. paper)
      I. Title.
      PS3614.E565L68 2010
      811'.6--dc22   2010034692

Design by Jennica Smith

Cover design by Sally Geier

Art direction by Lisa Bowden

Type is set in Avenir and Mrs. Eaves.

We express our gratitude to those who make Kore Press publications possible: The Tucson-Pima Arts Council, The Arizona Commission on the Arts, through appropriations from the Arizona State Legislature and the National Endowment for the Arts. Thanks to our readers and judge.

CONTENTS

I. *A Kindness*

II. *Love in New York*

III. Love and the Eye

IV. Light Is All We Ever See

Wine comes in at the mouth
And love comes in at the eye;
That's all we shall know for truth
Before we grow old and die.

—W. B. Yeats, from "A Drinking Song"

I.
A Kindness

The Speaker

Say your mother is working,
writing her dissertation down
in the library, down
in what they used to call
the cages, and the light is the light
of one bare scholarly bulb.
And your mother's
a raven-haired woman, a raven and
olive skinned, a terrible beauty.
And you are a little
terrible beauty, and she has put you up
on a shelf, while she writes, and say (as She
recounts it, now), a gentle somebody
happens by and asks, in the dark, and in a
whisper (because you are
so good, and so quiet), "Is that
a child or a doll?" What
do you say?

But it isn't, of course,
yours to answer; besides, you are,
in the moment, determined to be
both. So you follow the old
makers, the masters: you fashion
your mouth into and
after a small, bright 'o'
—as in *primrose*.

A Kindness

This morning I woke up angry at the Jehovah's
Witnesses. Why not go help
someone in actual need, I thought; or at least
go stand by a well, in case
a baby drops in. But I was kind to them
when they came; they were ladies and I
couldn't help it—the one
standing a little behind and staring
away to the side, down to the end
of the street, where surely
fields used to be; the other
doing the talking, bending a little, as if
she were pouring tea through the screen
door—what was it—something from
Matthew, something better than "Jesus is
Watching," and as she was talking I
was bending a little back, as in,
in return, because there was something about
the noon sun, beating the bare head
of the lady gazing away, that seemed
to demand it. These summer days—they are
so big, so empty, so blank that long-ago fields
can actually fill them, and you can stand
on a porch, and, staring, fill up the fields:
whether with flowers drowsing, or
workers in wavering heat, or children
in deep shade. What was the lady seeing?
Maybe the children, waving. Maybe
a cloud, coming.

The Walking Stick

1 / HISTORY

Today I took a big stick off a tree
And hit the tree with the stick
To make the stick mine and then

As I walked with it
Struck every rock within striking
Distance and even a few

That weren't—I hit
My way through the world—rocks,
Daisies, water, Oh

It felt good, it felt
Like a million years
And recording it all with each

Whack I thought
Tomorrow somebody might pick up
My stick, might turn

My stick in their hands and
Might even say to themselves
Something has happened here

2/THE SHADOW

This evening I called the stick Pearl
Because it looked old and elegant leaning
Against the white wall; because

In the quiet the stick was my great-
Grandmother Pearl's right leg—
Pearl of the ragged bible, Pearl of the soft

Back yard and the soft porch where the leg
Swung to the bible, predicted
A rain and dangled a black

Shoe. . . I knew her
One evening only. And only as tall as her thigh
I said to the stick,

Pearl, you can only be Pearl
For tonight—and only
By lamplight.

3 / THE SUNRISES

Oh Stick
We puffed our way up
The side of the mountain
Where you were born in the
Half dark, huffing, up
So early to see it, the sun
Rising, and scrambling
Over the rocks, daisies, water
                    —We
Did not want to miss it
Climbing is something we don't
Naturally do and we knew
We'd miss it, we knew
Still going, still grabbing for
Breath we've missed it
I said which was when
You gave me a swift
Kick in the pink and then
There it was
The sun coming up
All over again—do you
Remember? How it hit
The tops of our hearts: how
Its journey down
Started there?

4 / FULL MOON

Tonight the stick fell in love with itself
It lay on the carpet and acted
As much like a branch
As it could; it was awful to see it reaching
For sun and birds and needles—I said
Cut it out, I said Stick do you know
All your small round elbows, Stick
Do you know that the birds
Are not looking for you, or know
You bend like a tall girl's arm
When she's standing before her
Beloved, undressed, and in love. . .
And the stick fell in love
All over again, it lay there a while
And was quiet and then
I shut off the lamp and we lay there
Looking at all that light in the dark

5 / HOW IT ENDED

This morning I took the stick back
I put the stick down
Next to a creek I was going

To spend some time with it saying
Goodbye but this bee
Came out of nowhere

This bee that kept saying hey
Flower I know you're a flower you can't
Fool me you flower flower

Come back—but I
Was running, I ran
Like a stupid old woman and way

Way back behind me I heard
Not the stick
But a bird, laughing—

Landscape and Elegy

This morning the sun rose, and the people stirred.
Though in their stirring they couldn't
be seen—only the blue sky, and the white,
and the brick, and the lone cedar
hugging the side of their home. . .
After a death, after an old woman
(very old) is lowered into the ground, the sun
rises the same; the birds make
the same cacophony up in the tops
of the yards. And a Sunday looks
like a Sunday. One
wonders, maybe, a little bit more about
the stirring, the people across, waking—
the girl's foot's first touch
of the clean floor; or the father's opening one eye
and gently awaiting the other. . .
                                        She was lowered
slow as a beam, and with the same
angular, unresistable swing, left to right,
and again to the right, and in a pale blue robe
is how she was dressed. Though nobody saw except
the one who dressed her,
in a low room, while the sun rose.
It was early. And it was tender.

The Job

There was the evening in summer
a thousand mosquitoes
entered the guestroom and died

for lamplight: a thousand
black lace stars
hugging the white walls.

In the morning
they were looked in on and then
swept up, then carried

away and outside. The job
was done by a child.
And the room

was the same: guests
came and slept in it every
so often, as often the child

would dream about paper
catching fire and polite
ashes, like stars.

Sympathy

To you, cow
whose udder hung

like a heart out
of your back

end—valentine
to January's last

days, full
heart in the cold field's

somehow ongoing
air, part

miracle, part
garbage—I

started to offer
the big pink

carnation I carry
in all cold fields.

I usually offer it,
cow, well; but

you, you bent
and ate. The flower

was out too far.
And freezing.

You and your
purpling heart, eating

away—did you even
see me tip over?

Subdivision Diana

Evening, early.
Moon like a nail in the blue.
Not like the face
of the divine; these
days, that's
in the green grass and the lines
of fence, and fence.
The moon's a clipping, a wisp
of straw. A story. Once, maybe,
there was a girl, running. Once,
for certain, woods: enough for a
story: there was a girl
running, a wisp of straw coming
undone from her dark hair.
Sitting up there, the moon's
white, as a mark. I can't tell you
how bright, how golden
the neighborhood light.
While in her yard,
at practiced, determined
angles, this girl gives commands,
barking at nothing.
Aiming at air.

Little Bird

What is a child but dark.
What is a child, if not a pocket of dark.

A lark flew through the word and so
I loved it, when I was no more than a blot in it: *dark.*

Sometimes I think of the Romans, building their aqueducts and their arches,
    shining their heavy helmets,
then lying down on their cots, in the dark.

Petrarch loved Laura; that was a story I knew.
But loved her in sunlight, not shadow. Not in the dark.

Dreaming I walked in a German park; deer
fed from my hand. Childhood: silver and birchlight and lost to the dark.

Here is a memory: Istanbul, the great market, uncle looking
for symbols of love: a white gardenia, a golden pot in the dark.

For lying awake, they gave me a ceiling constellated with stars.
For lying awake is a battle fought with the dark.

One little bird—she passes part of the night in a high
corner, under the roof. How tightly she tucks herself in—gray dot on the dark.

Make me a promise: never grow out of the dark
you are. Keep off the light; bring me a thought on the dark.

The victor gets laurels, the bark cradle a final
push, and a song. It is hot in the tent. The song is soft. Then it's dark.

Twenty Answers

Because.
Because it is blue in the hills.
I'm not lonely.
Nor am I a river in Spain.
I'm the public.
To grieve is my occupation.
I am on occasion a body of fire.
Yes I'm happy to ride in the car.
I speak.
And the word for carnation is *sorry*.

I'm sorry.
I will not be sorry for long.
This is my lunchbox.
I'm headed for big, black ocean.
A Leo.
No.
My glasses have always been off.
It's the Fourth of July.
That's my sapphire.
The word—cut into my tongue—is for love.

The Sea

Last night in a dream, two dodo birds
stepped out of the sea.
They were mother and child. The sea
lined the edge of the room; it lapped
at the edge of the room, which wasn't
my room, nor the room
of anyone known to me, or remembered.
The dodos were holding hands.
And the eyes on the mother were like
Elizabeth Taylor's in *Cleopatra*: lined
and lavender. Lavender lined
with kohl. Or it may be
that the mother had just one eye—
it looked at me sideways: eye like the eye
suspended inside the pyramid
on the dollar. Whichever, she held fast
to the other, the littler dodo,
who beautifully stood there and blinked.

I want to reason the dream.
Someone I know, for example, is writing
a poem on the dodo—its glorious heavy
extinction; its feathers like blades
from a steel fan spangling
down the eons. But these—they stepped
from the sea so slowly, purposefully,
contentedly, even; somber as stones,
like supplicants come from the temple
of sheer silence, or sheer togetherness.
Dressed in dresses of brown cloth.

And the only sound was the sound
of the sea, blackly lapping away
at the floorboards. The eye
of the mother—it held fast to me.
Alice in Wonderland, maybe.
Or, my little study of
earliest glyphs; fishes and eyes
and a lot to decide: famine can mean
abundance; the field is fallow or sold;
from the word *dodo* two eyes look out
and examine the world. Or what about
my mother and her round mirror that
magnifies, down to the pore: up
in Virginia she's leaning into its
lighted rim while the room
darkens around her; the farm, the dream
darken around her.

But that is a sealess country. Unless
you think of the fields—not fallow, the way
in summer they glance and wave.
I have turned my back to her house
and been lost, at sea. And that, in fact,
was all: the dodos turned their backs
and retreated, into the sea.
Such tiny pointed ears they had.
Their hands were still clasped.
It could have been a field.

II.
Love in New York

Office Geraniums

In the sun, it is hot.
Not in the sun, it's cold. A bead
of sweat lives in your
sweater, for all October.

Someone's hauled geraniums
raised in the Adirondacks
here, to the office. They smell,
like shovels. You know

how people will say *We need
bodies—another body
here*, or just *more bodies*
for this, or that. How people

haul in geraniums, haul in
some plants, haul off wedding
pairs in carriages: bodies
with sun on their necks and

beads in their armpits,
for all life. Poor
geraniums, pretty in dirt.
They are at work.

Security Guard Reading in Sunlight

Think of all the objects we have in the world.
The books. The chairs. The pillows. The wide white
clothing solely for beds. The tinderboxes.
The cans, the lids, the albums, the racks, the animals made
of wicker. The towels, the antimacassars mended
by hand. The socks and bottles, clocks and mugs
and mirrors and strings; the telephones just
for children. The bikes and the knives, the platters, locks
and bells, collections of dolls, antlers and music
stands; the hooks, the doilies, the canes, all
heaped, one of these days, in the widest swath
of sunlight imaginable. Think, too, of the glittering
side of the ocean, of gulls flying like kites tied
to the mountain of so many things whittled or thumbed
or held. Of the man's finger, moving across the page
of his tome. Of the page itself, fluttering.

The Lovely Tall Novelist Danced

As if to annul
any suspicion
he was a saltine,

he danced
like a stick
thrown by some native

into a fiery
sunset. And went
on dancing

after the music
had stopped, which was
when the women

looked into their
drinks and saw
how stunning

olives become
when you do not
ignore them.

The Door

My love is the door the giraffes go through
when all the giraffes are at dinner
and there
is their door, in the hour
the old city sun comes down to light
the stone the door
was made from, with nothing in mind
but tallness.
It's five o'clock.
And it couldn't
be simpler: all giraffes inside, the door
and the hour make together a quiet
fineness, tall and on fire as I am
beside you, admiring a golden
door in a wall in an hour
all things blaze in, given
the weather is right, and the old sun
chooses to burn.

Gandhi's Ashes

I've watched so much TV, I have seen even
Gandhi's ashes, put on a boat and the boat
rolled down a paved hill and put
to sea, a sea of people

sending it in, after the fire
that publicly burned Gandhi's body.
...A sea of humanity mooned
the moment's narrator, a woman

wearing a flowery dress. It was hard
telling the ashes from all
the flowers, a sea of flowers
topping the cart that turned

into the boat that rolled
into the sea... *The sea.*
Really there is no such thing.
Except in the best of intentions.

Apartment Elegy

A table, a blue
glass pitcher. Flat

black of the table,
forget. The roundest

of blues, *forgive*.
Then a small rain;

then, silence, silence
like earthenware.

Silence for the first time
in a long

time, along with
the wainscot, the clean

wood corners, and,
in the curve of the pitcher's

handle, the ear
of the one who has gone.

Love in New York

Where I lived
in between the small
chair and lamp shops on East
Ninth Street, there was a woman
I never saw who lived
on the ground
floor of my building.

Her place
gave to the street and nearly
every night late
she was made love to by someone
who made her cry out, made her make
sounds like a child who'd fallen
into a well.

And people would
pass, outside, and the stoplights
would turn, red, and
red, and the lamps
burned in their shades;
as for the chairs, they waited
with open arms.

There was no one to save her.
No one to drown her, either.

Luscious Prayer

Lord, at the funeral let me not
perform for the crowd. Strike me down if I do—
you who have seen me rehearse on the necks
of friends that sadness that hangs, Lord,
like a sumptuous grape.
My lover is always dying, and greenly, sweetly I go
in those dreams to explode on the
broadest shoulder. Lord, let it

be over—not his life, but mine
on the lawn I go gushing
over and over across.
Refund, please, everyone's ticket.
I lick my lips of it.

Spring in New York

Because it was spring, winter's murders
rose to the banks
of the city's rivers. That bride-to-be

from the papers—revealed
at last, at Sunken
Meadow. Spring

revealed her, raising her light bones
to the cradling arms
of grass. And we never

actually saw her body—we saw
the grass, waving. The seemingly
sad reporter. Rain

falling on the reporter. A cloud
going by like a last
train out.

Downtown Love Letter

Where was it I left you—walking north
into the world of the avenue, after a burst
of rain—
The sunlight was brighter; the famed
bridge was blooming, the little flag
topping its tulip towers was flapping
city happiness: clean heaven over, dark
water under, streets blacker, air
blue as a lamb or a picture book—yes,
you were walking north: city of cloth
trundled, washed, flown, the sunlight
paper-bright; white paper: truly, it flew.

Death, Fifth Avenue

I saw two old women today
moving through time
through the huge

lobby of the building
I work in, through
the gold doors too

heavy to ever truly
open, or close.
They were moving

over the marble, slow
as flowers, past
the flowers forever

in bloom
inside: they were heading
on a diagonal toward

the elevator's open
doors. They were so old
I couldn't move.

They were so old
I wanted
water: so

beautifully and
intently were they
holding each other,

and everything
else in the whole
world, up.

III.
Love and the Eye

The Sleepers

Twice now, I've been to a poetry reading
here in the capital city. And twice
someone sitting near me's begun
to sleep, and, at length, to snore.
It's spring. I'm new here. Which isn't
exactly true—I grew up here, but now,
years later, I'm new enough
that the Capitol's dome looms
like a huge sweet when I cross
its path, walking. I stop, and look.
And at the readings I've stopped
hearing and looked with wonder on
the sleeper, elderly both
times, and earnest, earnest
both in presence and in sleep,
the head beginning its halting
nod downward to weightlessness,
toward the weightless dream
of sleep; then inhaling itself
back up, when the poet's voice
stopped, between poems, and silence
held the room a little too tightly
for sleep... Or when there was
a laugh, or really an elegant
cross-the-room snicker, which
is more and more often
these days.
                 But the dream
won out, both times; the head
found, both times, its place
on the chest, and finally oozed out
an original innocent song: I mean it:
a gentle snore.

These readings
take place at the dinner hour,
the hour between evening and
night, when the light is the color
of roses and in it the Capitol
sits, like an enormous cake.
And the monument and the memorials
glow on their own, and the planes
sink into National Airport; they drop
slowly as petals into a pink sea.
And the poets—the luminaries, the best
we have—read; and those of us who
have had a long day, or a long
life, begin, along with the sun,
and in the arms of voices possibly
tinted by God, to fall asleep.
This is the city of spring.
I knew that when I was a child.
And knew, like the sleepers, how
to ride away on a golden swing
into a day's end, my head sunk
over and over again in *A Child's
Garden of Verses...*

I know I romanticize
the failing body—not to mention
the failing light. But to return
home is, in a way, to forgive and
dignify, an older child looking to
sleep and dream deep in the tint
of a familiar bed. In spring the paths
leading up to the Capitol steps
are lined with tulips as tall, as red
as poppies. And at the readings'

ends, the ones who had slept
walked, with the rest of us, after
a cracker, some wine, into the lighted
night, finally wide awake and
nodding, agreeing that it was good.

God

God has found you out
my grandmother said
after finding
the well-rinsed cigarette butt
left on the edge of her lavender
basin. I burned
and tingled to think
she was God; she certainly
could have been Him
in her tight-necked tube
of a robe, coming fast
from the bathroom, backed
by the daylight in which
she'd been reading, holding
the butt out a good
foot in front of her
like a bad fish, her other
hand down.
That minute
is still lidded up like a jar
of something I wanted
then and there
preserved: the butt
a knot in my eye, the
burning, the love
of my grandmother coming
all pursed and straight;
straight as a baseball bat:
walking, believing.

The Cézanne

A bee came to die on a pillow.
It seemed to be seeking the decent rose
printed there, because
it let one of its legs
touch and touch the petal-edge, all
evening long, and into morning.
But what do I know of bees
or bees' seekings? Or of dying,
for that matter; can it be
as simple as this staying still,
hard by, or on, a
rendering one likes? Maybe I know
everything, as the woman did
who pressed her hands into her favorite
Cézanne and caused a scene.
⠀⠀⠀⠀⠀⠀⠀⠀Or as the bee
seems to do, turning now, compass-like, to
a redder edge. Humility's a sin
when it comes to roses' edges, or
a painting, or the end
of life. Or the day's beginning.

The Great Lawn

(Saratoga Springs)

The man looks like an archer his knee
Lunging forward his elbows
Expertly bent at the camera like fierce
Wings he aims his entirety at
The woman who leans
Girlishly back into her billowy
Dress and on the low wall and against
The air between her and the girl
Who is a statue and therefore truly
A girl her arms *en haut* in thanks

&

They set the child down like a toy and it goes
Straight to the low stone wall which it hits
Then back to the parents then back
To the fountain wall and water its arms
Aimed out of its body like picnic
Knives ready to stick the wide world
In the stomach the unbloody black
Water green trees green grass and im-
Perturbable marble girl while the parents
Kiss as if for the very first time

&

Some bridesmaids go by in slinky
Metallic dresses like young alligators their bags
Catching the light and deflecting
The light on the emerald
Grass it is early and they look a little

Hung over but still
They know where to go (to the garden
Of roses) and what they will do there and here
Comes the bride way behind them looking
Like a cosmetic puff one of them dropped

᠍ℰℙ

These children are dressed for rain they carry
Tiny umbrellas that match
Their coats one pink
One red the pink one is
Smaller they run and their adults
Glide in slowly behind them like swans
Or sliding stones not minding or not
Really feeling the rain after all
Their hearts are a few feet ahead of them
Running and screaming the words

ℰℙ

And here come the old in their green
Visors and still-folded clothes the grass
Is so good to them so soft
Under their canvas feet there are
Three of them man woman man and they don't
Look at the statue they don't
Need to they simply look down as they
Pass in front of her making the girl
Seem to soar like a white
Prayer for the woman who's missing

Snow

My lover
ground his black sneaker into the dirt and then *My love
for you*, he said, *is like civilization; it rises
and falls.* Downward he spoke and I looked
to the ground: all blue and waiting for
crocuses; cracks, dust, and now
snow, falling like ash, black
tip of his sneaker
boring the tiny
grave I nodding
got into.

Motel

Flat motel bed.
Flat brown
expanse. Car

outside and yet
another new life
doing its tanta-

lizing dance on the
ceiling. The iris
aimed and stripping.

Never undressing.
Just stripping.
While, outside, poolside,

some Mom, bored,
says it again.
I'm watching.

Maria Returns

("All My Children")

Today, all week, all summer,
dark Maria returns
to her husband, Edmund.
She has been dead five seasons.
But for Maria, turns out, death
was only a loss, and she returns
as a loss, standing among
the ferns in the park
of at last at last, alone
and holding a suitcase.
Few on my side of the track
would say how delicious
this is: the waiting
mostly for Edmund's expression
when he will see her again
for the first time, in the
stables, of all
places, the humblest of places,
we'd probably all agree, in the heat
of our houses, for love.
For reentry.
Maria will cross the straw.
Edmund will cross the straw.
Deep summer, all summer.
The hummingbirds ripping themselves
to and from the feeder.

The Hay Man

arrives rising, riding his blue
four-wheeler up and out
of the wide field.

He wears a blue shirt
to match. He's old,
we've heard, but good: a local

mower, one of the wonders of
the local world. He'll change
this world—a house

in a field—in a lingering
hour, and I wave
from the porch at the blue

glint that is him, over and
over again, goodbye. By tonight
our waving evenings will all

be baled and rolled, to the ends
of peripheral vision, away.
And the rest of the day,
all day, is the moment he's gone.

Love and the Eye

There you are: a sudden head
in a lake, at evening, when no one
should be in a lake, when the light is becoming
a weaving of gray
and darker gray. And on the shore, something's

perceptible, barely;
could be a small, possibly hunched-over
thing with a beating
heart; then, maybe,
a rock; then, slowly, faintly,

trousers: a pair
of trousers; the heart, my heart
slowing down to the old round
rhythm of recognition; the lake
now brightening under the brightening

moon, so that your head
in the water becomes
black and dear as a loon's cap; so that
the poor, faithful eye
works itself to a tear, following.

Lauderdale

At dusk, the grandmother sits alone
in the light of the long pale pool and speaks
to the frog who is waiting
by the electric gate of the clubhouse.

It will be all right, she says, leaning out
from her chair. Her voice

is churning, and old, and wet
with advice. Her newly red hair
purples under the bug light. *It will be
all right*, she says, again, and again

the sky rolls in and out on its journey
across the peninsula, rattling the palms.

IV.
Light Is All We Ever See

Pain

The mailman
is drunk.
It is spring. It
is spring and the mailman
is drunk, I see him
shaking his way down the wet
street from my window, which
is pretty. My

pretty window the mailman
is drunk in, out
in his slicker and bright
boots—did I say
it is raining? Rain
and the mailman
is drunk, and
eight, only eight
homes on this
street, and he
is crashing
into air
in the middle—

I love him
for this, love him
drunk, in rain,
in the green pain
oblivion is—

Is it
sick, or strange
placing myself
here, in the
story, his green
princess? I did
say it is
spring, and I
see him, and see
the new leaves,
slappy wet, begin
to make for the mailman
a frame: a frame
shaped like a leafy
heart, a heart
as leafy as if
he—

as if we
were, this raining
morning, happy.

The Lovers Smoking

They bolt up in bed, one of them runs
for an ashtray and matches, they sit up, light up
facing each other, draw, inhale,
exhale on their pushes of midnight
new-love wordsong: *I*
want, I hated,
I won't, I want—their spark-dots making a fast
graph in the dark, smoke
streaming from them like breath
out of horses into the woods at the bed's
cold edges; they light up
another, it cannot be done
quickly enough: sprint
of flame, his mother, her father, their plans
blow from their noses and wind up
over their heads, hanging important
sky they finally
fall asleep under, two
small, smelly gods.

Bobcat With Rat

(Durham Zoo)

A lovely young girl
with braids poses
beside a big bucket.

She puts
her hands on her hips.
Then, man-like, *He'll spit*

the stomach
onto the floor,
she says, sure

even the most
faraway piggybacked
child can hear her

explain. And then
the small man
in the cage

does what she says.
You can tell
he is used to it.

The Man

(On my birthday)

Just outside Tallahassee
I saw a man
manning a peanut stand.
REDNECK PEANUTS it said,
his stand, and the man—
he was leaning beside it—looked
like Hemingway, or Bluto,
or Captain Nemo.
He leaned, it seemed, on air:
on his own volume,
right by the two-lane road
slow with tourists traveling
south, and west, into Florida's
aqua thicket, towards
the crystal sea. He, it
could have been long ago;
it could have been the fifties.
It could have been a dream.
And my thought on the instant
was, in a hundred years—in
fifty, even—he—this man—
will be impossible: the sight—
a stand, speared and golden-
groved with Spanish Bayonet
and crayon letters, manned
by a heaven-uncle with a beard
and pipe (he had no pipe,
but he did)—will be
impossible. Everywhere

the water lurked; flashed
behind each scrubby tree;
behind the signs for crossing bears
(that black-on-yellow pair)
like a vision; and along we all crawled
to meet it: what we barely see
but know is there to buoy us,
then bury us. I should have stopped
—I wish I'd stopped—but I was
traveling, south, and in a line;
already turned to salt, that air.

Bells For Ruth

There was a young cook
who dressed in black for his sister's
wedding and took his four
sauté pans along. At the end

of the day, after the long
reception (at which he
concocted all the sauces),
after the long tear cried

out of his mother's
good eye, he went home,
alone, and hung his pans
back on the wall; then

saw, in their flat
silver and blackened
bottoms, the sun
go down, four times.

Oracle

My mother and father walked through a cave
in Greece. I wasn't born, but I was there,
and I have a mental picture of this.
My mother is leading, hoping something
from all her reading will burn into being
before her. My father is following her,
taking his tall frame with care along
the passage, using his large hands now
and again to steady himself. My mother
is hoping, too, something for me: wishing
there, in the sacred dark, that I will be
something other than an accountant, a clerk,
or a wife. She concentrates—maybe she
closes her eyes. This is the sixties, and so
everything's black and gray, and roseate
brown, and at the other end the light
my mother and father are moving toward
is a simple, pure, chalk white—not
the blare of a vision, not the bright
feather of a god. They're moving along,
and if I close *my* eyes, even the dark
is plain: no shape, no figure, other than
theirs, in the grain appearing. There
is my father: his camera strap a fine
leather, a line forever dividing
his chest. And my mother: her back
to my father, walking with me.
Her hair is as black as the Caspian Sea.

In the Jewish Cemetery

Childhood is like the hibiscus
next to the garbage can, wide opening cone

you miss though it's there, white ear
with lavender hole, so close

to your cheek. My mother leaned over and told me
it was too sacred

to bomb. So I took in,
took with me the old stones, their

marks, the walls that closed in, the fact
that what was left over over the graves

was the piece of the sky they lay
quietly under, periwinkle in color. My mother

was very beautiful, always in navy,
Givenchy, Dior, smelling of ribbed

sweaters and flowers and sometimes telling a thing
so deeply into my ear it would begin

to bloom there. And when we were there
it was twilight, as it is now, and I am

alone in the yard. Or
almost alone, in the yard.

Light Is All We Ever See

Sometimes there is a man
outside the gas station, standing
under the telephone pole, in the light,
with the rest of the night
heaving right next to him like
a tiger, or elephant.

But he doesn't want it, the night—
nor the moon nor the couple of cats
yowling around in the luminous
shadow-bath of the parking lot.

Which is where
a house used to be and now
a parking lot line divides lit
from unlit, and you can watch the man
in his absolute choice
to be lit, so that he becomes, in his
shining jacket, every
golden fly of your thought.

But he doesn't want that, either—
the thought—nor even the light:
look how he's low, hiding, darkening himself
in brightness; hunkered as if
of a sudden a great love
were beside him, just come to earth,
still roiling from the long journey.

The Idea of Love

Isn't it mixed, anyway, into love
Already—just the idea, the high idea—
The incomplete image, at night, to music,
Stereo light like a lamp
Set in a window?

Storm, come: that's the idea:
Turn the suburban squares
To a broody sea; dress me in gray;

And I will walk to the ships
All night, whatever that means; I

Will walk to the ships, all night.

The Mailbox

For a minute, you
disappear. The front yard
is that dark. You walk

down the walk and are
gone, the way a person
walking into heaven in a movie

goes into smoke and the smoke
closes, seamless.
The trees in the yard

are young: all breeze and
bend, no trunks
to people the dark. Stars

I don't know, never
have, and there is no moon.
All I know

is the mailbox, big
and white on its pole, and
shining, so much

like a mailbox it must
be something else: a
tree, a star, or the moon

in the place you are
this minute.
Love, with dark, does this.

Notes

1. "Twenty Answers" responds to Donald Justice's poem "Twenty Questions".

2. "The Sea" owes a debt to poet Christina Matthews.

Acknowledgments

Grateful acknowledgment is made to the editors of the following publications, who published poems from this collection, some in slightly different versions:

The Atlantic Monthly ("Pain", "The Lovely Tall Novelist Danced")
Best New Poets 2007 ("In the Jewish Cemetery")
Black Warrior Review ("The Idea of Love")
Poetry ("Lauderdale", "Maria Returns")
Stand (U.K.) ("The Cezanne", "The Lovers Smoking", "The Sleepers")
Stillpoint ("Office Geraniums", "Spring in New York")
TriQuarterly ("The Walking Stick")
Tsunami ("God")
Zone 3 ("Subdivision Diana")

"Office Geraniums" also appears in the anthology *Urban Nature: Poems about Wildlife in the City* (Milkweed Editions).

Grateful acknowledgment also to the Corporation of Yaddo, the writing communities at Warren Wilson College and Georgia College, and to the tireless friends of this work, especially Jonathan Blunk, Alice Friman, Miller Oberman, Andrea Werblin, and Alan Williamson.

Thanks to Lisa Bowden and the staff at Kore Press.

And very special thanks to Claudia Rankine, for seeing it.

About the Author

Laura Newbern comes from two long lines of Arkansans, was born in Germany, and grew up in Washington, D.C. She holds degrees from Barnard College, New York University, and the MFA Program for Writers at Warren Wilson College. An Associate Professor of English at Georgia College & State University, Newbern serves as the Poetry Editor of *Arts & Letters*. She is a recipient of a 2010 Writer's Award from The Rona Jaffe Foundation.

About the Press

As a community of literary activists devoted to bringing forth a diversity of voices through works that meet the highest artistic standards, Kore Press publishes women's writing that deepens awareness and advances progressive social change.

Kore has been publishing the creative genius of women writers since 1993 in Tucson, Arizona, to maintain a more equitable public discourse and establish a more accurate historic record.